PRAYING
WITH POWER

How to Engage in a Deeper Level of
Personal Prayer by Praying the Scriptures

by

Bruce Hills

CHI
BOOKS

CHI–Books,
PO Box 6462, Upper Mt Gravatt,
Brisbane, QLD 4122, Australia

www.chibooks.org
publisher@chibooks.org

Praying with Power
How to Engage in a Deeper Level of
Personal Prayer by Praying the Scriptures

Print ISBN: 978-0-9875608-0-3
eBook ISBN: 978-0-9875608-1-0

Printed in Australia, United Kingdom and the United States of America.

Distributed in the USA and Internationally by Ingram Book Group and Amazon.

Also available from: www.bookdepository.co.uk and other outlets like Koorong.com in Australia.

Distribution of eBook version: Amazon Kindle, Apple iBooks, Koorong. com and others like Wesley Owen (UK), Barnes & Nobel NOOK, Sony eReader and KOBO.

Editorial assistance: Anne Hamilton
Cover design: Dave Stone
Layout: Jonathan Gould

CONTENTS

Foreword

Bruce Hills' book, *Praying with Power - How to Engage in a Deeper Level of Personal Prayer by Praying the Scriptures*, is a little "gold mine." It is short, clear and simple, yet practical and profound in its scope on praying the Scriptures.

The Holy Spirit inspired the Word. In order to pray the Word, the believer (both new and older), need to read the Word. The Holy Spirit can only draw upon the Word that is in your heart in order to pray back that Word - the Scriptures - to the Father.

In this book, Bruce gives you the "how to!"

Read it! Be challenged by it! Be blessed by it! And above all, do it!

May the Lord bless this book to the Body of Christ.

Kevin J. Conner
Author and Teacher, Melbourne, Australia

INTRODUCTION

Through Jesus' sacrifice and high priestly ministry, every Christian has bold and confident access to God in prayer anywhere and at any time. God invites and welcomes people to a deeper relationship with him through prayer. There are many components of prayer such as petition, intercession and thanksgiving. One of the least understood and often overlooked expressions of prayer is 'praying the Scriptures'.

Praying the Scriptures, as the phrase suggests, is actually using the words of Scripture as the content or basis of our prayer to God. But the practice is a lot deeper and more meaningful than simply repeating the words of Scripture in parrot fashion. It involves delving into the Word of God and allowing the Word of God to delve into us. It requires us to immerse ourselves in Scripture until Scripture permeates our prayers. It is finding in the words of Scripture the words that we cannot conceive in our own minds to express our praise or prayer to God.

There are depths and dimensions of prayer. Through its intentional integration with God's Word, praying the Scriptures leads us from the shallows of superficial prayer to a potentially deep place of intimately discovering God in fresh and profound ways.

Over its three chapters this book will cover three aspects of praying the Scriptures. The first chapter will outline nine principles that undergird the basis for *why* a Christian should pray the Scriptures.

Chapter two will explore five different ways of *how* we can pray the Scriptures. Then chapter three will suggest a number of *practical* ways in which we can learn to develop the practice of praying the Scriptures.

This book calls and challenges us to go deeper in prayer by embarking on the adventure of praying the Scriptures. My own prayer is that these principles will transform every reader's engagement with God through prayer.

CHAPTER ONE

Why Pray the Scriptures?

Before beginning to explore the practicalities of how to pray the Scriptures, I will propose nine compelling biblical reasons why we should pray the Scriptures.

First, praying the Scriptures is a way by which we can **discover more of God Himself through His Word**. The Word of God is the written revelation *of* God and *from* God (2 Timothy 3:16; 2 Peter 1:20–21). The Scripture *reveals* God's nature, activity, ways, works and words. The Bible is not a dead, dry or irrelevant historical book, but the living, vibrant and applicable Word of God to our lives today.

God still speaks through what he has spoken in his Word. The truth of Scripture is eternal truth. The principles of God's Word are unchanging principles. One of the ways we experience God as he has revealed himself in the Bible is by praying the Scriptures.

In mid–January 2012 a colleague and I had been teaching at a pastor's seminar in the north eastern Indian state of Assam. While being driven to Guwahati airport we encountered heavy traffic moving at a turtle's pace. Our trip had already been delayed and we were becoming concerned that we may miss our flight. If we missed this connecting flight we would miss our flight home to Australia from Delhi. On the surface of things there seemed to be no possible way that we would get to the airport in time.

Suddenly the Scripture came into my heart about God opening the Red Sea to deliver his people from Pharaoh and his army. Based on this Scripture, I prayed, 'Lord, as you miraculously opened the Red Sea, please make a way through this impassable traffic.' Within minutes of finishing my prayer I heard the distinct sound of sirens. I looked behind me and saw a motorcade of police and government vehicles driving on the wrong side of the road (which is not uncommon in India) also heading in our direction, presumably toward the airport. Cars merged left to allow the officials to get through. Once the last vehicle in the motorcade had passed, our quick thinking driver spontaneously swung in behind them to effectively join the motorcade. Despite being terrified by how erratically our driver drove, we made it to the airport significantly faster than if we had driven on the same roads without traffic. In fact, we were quite early for our flight. God had made a way where there was seemingly no way.

This answer to a prayer based on Scripture brought a renewed sense to my life that God was a God of supernatural deliverance. I can now emphatically say with unshakable confidence, 'He is a God who can make a way where there is no way!'

Praying the Scriptures bases our prayers on the revelation of God in his Word which, when God answers, brings the God of the Bible into the reality of our lives and circumstances. Consequently we receive a greater understanding and comprehension of God and His ways.

Secondly, praying the Scriptures is a way in which we can **apply** and **appropriate the Word of God** to our lives. Praying the Scriptures is a means of putting God's Word into practice. James wrote in his epistle that believers are not just to 'hear' or 'know' the Word of God, but actually '*do what it says*' (James 1:22). The author of Hebrews urged his readers to imitate mature Christians who constantly 'use' the Word of God as a way to spiritually discern good from evil (Hebrews 5:14).

Toward the end of the Sermon on the Mount, Jesus told a parable comparing two builders (Matthew 7:24–27). One he described as 'wise', the other as 'foolish'. Both men 'heard' Jesus' words, but it was only the 'wise' builder who put Jesus' words 'into practice'. Subsequently when natural disasters (such as rain, flood and wind) struck both homes, it was only the wise man's home which remained unscathed. Jesus explained why. It was because his 'foundation' was more secure and stable—it was on 'rock'. The foundation of 'rock' in this parable was not only 'hearing' Jesus' words but 'putting them into practice'.

In late July 2010 I began serving in a Mission's Agency as the International Director of Leadership Development. In the previous 25 years of full–time ministry, I had always been a salaried staff member in large churches, both as a team member and as a senior Pastor. Once I joined the Mission, however, I had to raise my own support and depend entirely on God for our income. This was very confronting because I don't like talking about money, preaching about money or raising money.

Of course, I knew all the Scriptures about God being 'Jehovah Jireh' ('The Lord our Provider' as in Genesis 22:14). As a preacher, I could also recite Philippians 4:19: 'And my God will meet all your needs according to his glorious riches in Christ Jesus.' I believed these verses. I preached and taught about them, but once I joined the Mission I had to *apply* these words of Scripture. I began the task of seeking to raise our

> **Praying the Scriptures is a way of putting God's Word into practice**

monthly support, but it was accompanied by earnest prayer, based on these and many other Scriptures relating to God's provision. God was incredibly faithful. Our initial year's support came within three months, which I was told was a record within the Mission. We have subsequently lacked for nothing. Raising support is an ongoing challenge, but I wouldn't change living by prayerful faith for anything. It's so exciting (and scary).

In applying this point more specifically, praying the Scriptures is a way of putting God's Word into practice. It is one thing to know God's Word, but quite another to apply it.

Thirdly, praying the Scriptures **bases our prayers on the Word of God**. Our prayers are most effective when they are grounded on Scriptural principles.

I was a youth pastor back in the mid–1980s, a time when I had much longer and darker hair than I do today. One Saturday night, one of the young ladies in the youth group asked me a question, 'Pastor Bruce, I have an unsaved boyfriend. I know he's about to propose to me. I have been asking God whether it is his will to marry him, but he is not speaking to me about it. What should I do?'

I suggested that we should see what the Bible says. I turned to 2 Corinthians 6:14–18 and asked her to read it aloud. Among other things it says, (v. 14) 'Do not be yoked together with unbelievers.' Once she'd finished reading all the verses I asked her what she felt those verses were saying to her. After a few minutes of quietly absorbing the implications of the passage she looked at me with a very sad expression and conceded, 'It means I shouldn't be marrying him. I belong to Jesus, but he doesn't. Even though we're attracted to each other, have a lot in common and love each other, if we're not spiritually compatible then it won't work.' I nodded in silent agreement before sympathetically asking, 'What are you going to do?' She reluctantly answered, 'I need to break it off.'

Tragically, this story didn't have a happy ending. She ignored the counsel of Scripture and chose to marry the young man. In the process she withdrew from the youth group and church. About a year later she walked up to me with tears flowing down her face. 'I wish I had listened to you,' she said between sobs. The marriage had broken down. They had separated and filed divorce proceedings.

She would have saved herself a lot of unnecessary grief if she had first of all searched the Scriptures to find the Bible's instructions.

By way of application, may we, too, enquire into God's Word to find out what it teaches so we can lay a solid foundation for our prayers.

Fourthly, praying the Scriptures is a way of **reminding ourselves of what God has said in his Word**. We often have such short or selective memories. In the Old Testament, especially in Deuteronomy, one of the things that God continually told the Israelites to do was to *remember* all the things he had said and done (see Deuteronomy 6:12; 8:2; 18–19; 15:15; Psalm 103:2; 105:5). In this way they would remember him and how to live their lives according to his words and laws. Similarly, praying the Scriptures is a way of reminding ourselves and remembering what God has said and what God has done.

A vivid Scriptural example of this is when the people of Judah were threatened with annihilation by an alliance of armies (2 Chronicles 20:1). Alarmed, the people gathered outside the temple in Jerusalem where King Jehoshaphat stood and prayed for divine intervention. His prayer was a response to God's *specific* promise to Solomon *100 years before* that his '…eyes will be open and my ears attentive to the prayers offered in this place' (2 Chronicles 7:15; cf. 20:8–9). Jehoshaphat remembered the promise and used it as basis for his heartfelt prayer.

Late in 1998 my Dad was told that he would need an immediate quadruple bypass on his heart. He had been such a strong, healthy

> Praying the Scriptures becomes our response to what God has said in His Word

and vigorous man all his life that the prospect of an operation was unsettling. The heart specialist had given him firm instructions to rest because his heart was in a precarious state. While contemplating his surgery one night he was reflecting on Scripture when he read Psalm 73:26: 'My flesh and my heart may fail, but God is the strength of my heart and my portion forever.' This verse gave him an immediate assurance that he would come through the procedure, live a long life and have a productive ministry. His prayers from this point about his operation were based on this Scripture.

Likewise, praying the Scriptures reminds us of God's promises in his Word, especially those given as part of the new covenant (like 1 John 1:9; 2 Corinthians 5:17). In the same way that Jehoshaphat's prayer was a response to God's promises, so praying the Scriptures becomes our response to what God has said in His Word.

Fifthly, praying the Scriptures is a way by which we **express** and **exercise** our **faith in God**.

Faith in God must be based on the Word of God. If faith is not built on the Word of God, it can never stand the storms and tests of life. Faith is a response to the revelation of God in his written Word (2 Timothy 3:16; 2 Peter 1:21) and through His Son, Jesus Christ, the living Word of God (John 1:1–2; 14). Faith comes by hearing the Lord Jesus speaking to our hearts by the Holy Spirit through his Word (Romans 10:17). A study of the 'heroes' of faith in Hebrews 11 shows they all received a specific 'word' from God which formed the basis of their faith.*

---

* Some of the thoughts in this paragraph are adapted from Kevin Conner, *The Foundations of Christian Doctrine*, Vermont, Victoria: Acacia Press, 1980, p. 257.

As we pray the Scriptures we are saying, in essence, 'I believe in you as the Living and Eternal God. I believe in your Son, Jesus Christ, as the Saviour and Redeemer of the world. I believe your Word is divinely inspired and is unchanging truth. I believe in your sovereign rule and providence. I now pray based on Scripture because I believe your word to be completely trustworthy and true. I pray because my faith is in you.'

In response to very clear guidance from the Lord in late 2011, my wife and I made the decision to relocate back to our home town, Melbourne, after 12 ½ years living in sunny Brisbane. Consequently, we put our house on the market, not realising that at the time the Australian housing market was depressed. I was full of faith, however, that the home would sell quickly. I strongly believed that because our decision was based on unambiguous guidance, we were not under the jurisdiction of the market, but the jurisdiction of the Kingdom of God. However, after 90 days on the market and only one offer within the vicinity of our bottom line, traces of discouragement filled my heart.

Discouragement subtly fuels doubt. Doubt can have a corrosive effect upon our spiritual life. Doubt, if left unchecked or unaddressed, inevitably degenerates into unbelief. Unbelief is dangerous because it undermines faith in God. Without consciously realising it, my faith was being suffocated by unbelief.

Against that backdrop, I was drinking a very enjoyable coffee one morning while reading the devotional passage of Scripture designated for that day. It was the account of Balaam's second oracle to Balak (Numbers 23:13–26), where Balaam uttered, (v. 19) 'God is not a man, that he should lie, nor a son of man, that he should change his mind. Does he speak and then not act? Does he promise and not fulfil?' These words about the unchanging nature and character of God and his purposes exploded in my heart like combustible fuel. The word of God had illumined my heart, unmasked the unspoken unbelief and reignited faith. Responding to this verse, I spoke out

> **Faith—if it is to be legitimised as authentic faith—must be based on the Word of God**

loud to myself and to God, 'You are not flesh and blood, Lord, so you do not and cannot lie. You are God, so you do not change your mind. If you have said something, it will come to pass. I believe this.'

Something immediately shifted in my heart. My faith was restored and resolved. I knew the house *would* sell despite the market. It was no longer a question of *if* but *when*. Obviously, other factors known to God alone were at play behind the scenes. I just had to patiently (something that doesn't come naturally to me) trust that his timing would be perfect. From that moment on my prayers for the sale of the house were rooted in the teaching embedded in Numbers 23:19 that God does not lie, does not change his mind, but does fulfil his promises.

The house still didn't sell straightaway. In fact, it was a further four frustratingly long weeks. Looking back now I can see *why* the sale was delayed. Many things transpired during the *delay* that will be so important to our future lives. The biggest lesson I learned, though, was that our faith—if it is to be legitimised as authentic faith—must be based on the Word of God.

Sixthly, praying the Scriptures is a way to **memorise Scripture** or, in different words, to get the Word of God into our hearts (see Psalm 119:11; 1 John 2:14). The more we pray Scripture, the more of the Word of God fills the 'well' of our lives. Praying the Scriptures is a way to move the Scriptures from a cerebral knowledge of a particular verse or passage into a working knowledge within our hearts.

The Word of God in our hearts provides:

- illumination to the path on a dark night (Psalm 119:105)

- nourishing food for maturity (Hebrews 5:11–6:3; Deuteronomy 8:3; Matthew 4:4)

- preservation from wilful sin (Psalm 119:11)

- a spiritual weapon to resist the tempter and temptation (Matthew 4:1–11 'It is written')

- victory over evil and the evil one (1 John 2:14)

- growth (1 Peter 2:2)

- inward discerning between soul and spirit (Hebrews 4:12)

- exposure of our true motives (Hebrews 4:12)

- a mirror to show what we should be and should do (James 1:23–25)

Paul wrote to the church in Ephesus that the Word of God is part of our armoury in spiritual warfare (Ephesians 6:17), therefore memorising Scripture is a way to arm ourselves with verses we can deploy when attacked or tempted by Satan (Matthew 4:1–11). Additionally, memorised Scripture fills our inner well with resources the Spirit can draw upon to speak to us in critical moments when we need encouragement or guidance. In a similar vein, memorised Scripture can be quickened to us by the Spirit as a word of encouragement or counsel through us to bless others.

As a Pastor I have visited many people in hospital. At times, the circumstances were heartrending, tragic or life–threatening. I needed great wisdom in what I said because in most situations people were looking to me as their shepherd for words of hope. While it is appropriate to bring general words of comfort from Scripture, I would always pray and ask God to give me a specific Scripture for that circumstance. One day I received a call from a distraught father in the church I was leading. His young daughter had been rushed to hospital with a mystery disease that was having a devastating, potentially fatal, effect on her health.

I quietly prayed as I went in to see them. As I left the hospital lift heading toward their ward, the Holy Spirit reminded me of Lamentations 3:22–24 where it says (in part), 'Because of the Lord's great love we are not consumed, for his compassions never fail. They are new every morning; great is your faithfulness.' The message of these verses is that God will not allow the prevailing circumstance to overwhelm us. God's mercy (compassion and grace) are unfailing. As the sun rises each morning, so God's heart and acts of compassion are renewed to us day by day. All of this is grounded in God's faithfulness.

I shared the verses with the parents as they gathered around the child's bed. These verses (Lamentations 3:22–24) are a great comfort to anyone at any time, but on that day they were God's specific words to that specific family in that specific circumstance that he would bring the daughter through her health challenges one day at a time. That is exactly what happened. I regularly rang the family for updates and was thrilled to consistently hear of the progressive restoration of her health. Within months she had fully recovered.

This story could only be told because faithful Sunday School teachers challenged me as a child (sometimes with edible, sugar–filled incentives) to memorise the Word of God. I am indebted to them for building the discipline of memorising Scripture into my life. Praying the Scripture is one of the practical ways of putting verses to memory.

Seventhly, praying the Scriptures is a way to train ourselves to **go to the Word of God in times of need or crisis**. For some inexplicable reason, many Christians stop or reduce their praying and reading of Scripture during difficult times. Consequently they weaken and wither, whereas Scripture instructs them to persevere, specifically in faith–filled and single–minded prayer, such as for wisdom (James 1:2–8; 12). In seasons of trial or test, Christians are encouraged to:

- anchor themselves in the Word of God

- draw their strength from the Scripture
- fill themselves with what God has said in his Word
- pray the Scriptures in heartfelt responsive prayer
- trust in the nature, character and power of God as revealed in Scripture

Around the middle of 2007 I was having my weekly meeting with our Pastor for Worship and Creative Arts (WACA). She had made a decision and thought it may have ramifications so she wanted to run it past me. One of the backing vocalists in the young adult's program had been moonlighting as a contestant in a bikini competition being run at major car racing events on the Gold Coast. The WACA pastor felt that she shouldn't be in the music team while she was competing in a bikini competition. She was justifiably concerned that this sent mixed messages about what we stood for. On that basis she had decided to ask the young lady to stand aside from her singing duties in the young adult ministry while the competition was running.

To me, a young Christian lady parading her body around in front of ogling men was not consistent with Christian propriety or modesty. I was not making a judgment about whether a Christian lady should wear a bikini or not, nor was I making a judgment about the young lady's character. I was concerned that having her singing on the church platform could be interpreted as an endorsement of her extra–curricular activities. The truth was that we could not endorse it for numbers of reasons, so I completely supported the WACA pastor's decision.

The following week I was contacted by a reporter from a national current affairs TV program known for its tacky and truthless reporting. The mother of the aforementioned young lady had rung them to say that I had thrown her out of the church, which was completely untrue. Because the story was going to air whether I responded or not, I reluctantly agreed to an interview on camera to explain the facts and defend our position.

I thought the interview went well. I was measured and thoughtful in my responses, carefully explaining that we had *not* asked her to leave the church at all, but merely to step down from the music team while she was competing. I worded my justifications in everyday language rather than Biblical language. The reporter seemed quite satisfied and said his producers would have to decide whether to air the segment or not.

Nothing happened for some months so I assumed they had decided that it was not worth broadcasting. Six months after the interview, short excerpts of my interview appeared on the show's advertisements. On a particular Monday night in December 2007 the story aired. The unscrupulous reporter had knowingly and wilfully misrepresented me. Through deceptive and selective editing they had distorted my words and used different answers to different questions. The episode portrayed us as a legalistic, discriminatory and bigoted church. The next day we received dozens of nasty messages on the church's answering service and through email.

Even though the church was incredibly supportive and galvanised around me, the public antagonism unexpectedly affected me quite deeply. I went to the Scripture and reflected on Shadrach, Meshach and Abednego's uncompromising attitude to legislated idolatry (Daniel 3). These three young men refused to bow the knee because they knew that to do so would violate the second commandment to '…not bow down to [idols] or worship them…' (Exodus 20:5). They were, technically, guilty. Far from withering or capitulating, the three stood their ground. What struck me was that their faith didn't prevent the fiery furnace but preserved them *in* the middle of it. This story really encouraged my faith and strengthened my determination that we would not wilt under public pressure (our fiery furnace). These verses

> **Praying the Scriptures becomes a tangible way of trusting in the Lord**

undergirded the decision we had made—despite its cost. We would not bow down. Daniel 3 became the Scriptures around which I prayed throughout that whole trying week.

Searching the Scriptures in challenging times is a way of turning *to* God in dependency, faith and expectation. As we do so, praying the Scriptures becomes a tangible way of *trusting in the Lord* (Proverbs 3:5).

Eighthly, praying the Scriptures is a way by which we can **resist the devil in times of temptation and attack**. Matthew 4 and Luke 4 record the temptation of Jesus in the wilderness. On three recorded occasions Satan tried to tempt Jesus. In one instance the devil even quoted, actually misquoted, Scripture as part of his attempt to entice Jesus to sin (Luke 4:10–11; cf. Psalm 91:11–12).

Responding to each temptation Jesus replied, '*It is written...*' before proceeding to quote from Scripture (Luke 4:4, 8, 12). Jesus declared the Word of God as a means of confronting and rejecting the devil's temptation. Likewise, if we are to overcome the tempter and temptation, we must learn the principle of using the Word of God as part of the process of resisting.

Importantly, even though Satan is seen in Scripture as a 'tempter' (Matthew 4:1–14), not all temptation is exclusively or personally from him. As James 1:13–15 teaches, the common *source* of temptation is the innate evil tendency of human nature. Temptation in itself is not sin. It is what we do with temptation that determines if it becomes sin or not. Temptation is not irresistible or insurmountable (1 Corinthians 10:13). It *can* be defeated and resisted by drawing on the Spirit's indwelling strength, exercising will power to resist evil impulses (Romans 8:13; Titus 2:11–14) and deploying the Word of God as a mighty defence. Added to this is Jesus' own teaching on the important place of prayer in denying temptation (Matthew 6:13).

Throughout his letters, Paul metaphorically described the Christian experience in terms of warfare:

- The 'Church' is depicted as an 'army' (Ephesians 6:10–18)
- 'Enemies' are portrayed as 'spiritual forces' (Ephesians 6:12)
- 'Protection' is seen in terms of the 'armour of God' (Ephesians 6:10–18)
- 'Satan's attacks' are described as 'schemes' (2 Corinthians 2:11) and 'fiery darts' (Ephesians 6:17)
- 'Gospel ministry' is likened to ancient siege warfare (2 Corinthians 10:3–5)
- 'Weapons' are designated as having 'divine power to demolish strongholds' (2 Corinthians 10:4)
- 'Faith' is regarded as 'the good fight' (1 Timothy 1:18; 6:12)

The passage in which Paul employs the military metaphor the most is Ephesians 6:10–18 where he taught:

- The enemy of the church does not consist of 'flesh and blood' like those of Old Testament Israel, but 'rulers, authorities, powers and the spiritual forces of evil in the heavenly realms' (v. 12)
- These spiritual powers are demonic beings which are powerful, wicked and strategically-placed (vv. 11–13)
- The leader of these powers is 'the devil' whose 'schemes' they carry out against the church (v. 11)

Paul revealed that the devil's evil power, influence and work against Christians are not random, indiscriminate or whimsical, but covert, intentional and planned. He uses the word 'schemes' (wiles, tricks) of the devil—a word that speaks of strategy and deception. Some translators liken the word 'schemes' to the English word 'stratagem' which is generally regarded as a manoeuvre designed to deceive or outwit an enemy in war. Satan uses evil tactics to oppose, derail or divide the church.

The question then becomes, 'How can we stand strong against the attacks of such enemies?' On the surface it seems that we are often weak and ignorant of what is taking place in the spiritual realm. Nevertheless Christians are instructed to take their stand against these schemes by being strong and firm in the Lord (vv. 10, 11, 13), by clothing themselves in the 'armour of God' (vv. 14–17; cf. Isaiah 59:17) and by adopting a vigilant attitude of prayer (v. 18).

Just after the fall of communism in the former Soviet Union, a newspaper published a particularly sad letter written by a Russian mother whose son had been killed on the frontline in a fierce battle in Chechnya. Her son was a potato farmer conscripted for national service into the Russian military. Due to budget cuts and restrictions his unit of conscripts was unable to use *live* ammunition during their basic training. For some absurd reason this lady's son, along with a newly formed battalion of conscripts, was sent to the front to face hardened Chechnyan nationals fighting for independence from Moscow. Because he was drastically ill–prepared and poorly trained, he was killed within hours. The Russian mother was, understandably, devastated and angry with the military hierarchy for sending her son without adequate training.

The 'son' in this account parallels many Christians who do not know their spiritual weapons or how to use them. Consequently they live in defeat to the ravages of temptation and satanic attack.

Linking Paul's thoughts on the 'Word of God' being the 'sword of the Spirit' (Eph. 6:17) and the importance of watchful prayer (v. 18), the application is that praying the Scriptures would be a vital and powerful part of a Christian's

> The shape and timing of answered prayer depend entirely upon the purposes, prerogative and providence of God

arsenal in spiritual warfare. Prayer which stems from God's Word is a way by which Christians can prevail in this otherworldly conflict.

Ninthly, **God answers prayer**. One of the foundational reasons why we should pray the Scriptures is because God has revealed himself as a prayer–answering God (Psalm 91:15). He doesn't always answer in the way we may expect or desire. God has eternal plans and purposes that transcend human understanding (Isaiah 55:8–9). The shape and timing of answered prayer depend entirely upon the purposes, prerogative and providence of God.

In the Scripture there are a number of verses suggesting that some answers to prayer are assured. In each case, however, there are very clear conditions mentioned in these verses that govern answers to prayer. We'll briefly examine four main references and investigate the particular condition necessary for answers to prayer and the relationship to praying the Scriptures.

A first condition to answered prayer is located in the wonderful promise written by the apostle John in 1 John 5:14–15 that '*if*' (and it is a big 'if') '...*we ask anything according to his will, he hears us. And if we know that he hears us—whatever we ask—we know that we have what we asked of him.*' In this context, answers to prayer are contingent upon them being aligned to God's will. One of the profound mysteries of prayer is summed up in the question, 'How do I know what I am praying is the will of God?' God's will and God's ways are recorded in his Word; that is, the Scriptures prescribe the way the Lord wants us to live and how he wants things done. If our prayers are based on the clear teaching of a Scripture, they are more likely to conform to God's will. As someone has well said, 'All true prayer is an adaptation of the one prayer: "*your will be done.*"' Therefore praying the Scriptures is a way of aligning our prayers with the will of God.

A second condition to answered prayer is found in John 15:7 in Jesus' teaching: 'if you remain in me and my words remain in you, ask whatever you wish, and it will be given you' (cf. 1 John 3:24). Employing the allegory of vine, branches and fruitfulness, Jesus said that we would receive answers to prayer *if*

(a) we live reliant on the indwelling life of Jesus in the same way as a branch draws nutrition from a vine, and

(b) we obey, apply and feed upon the teaching of Jesus.

Using Scripture as a basis for our prayers is one of the ways in which Jesus' words become part of us. If we 'live in him and his words live in us' we can have the confidence that our prayers will be listened to and acted upon.

A third condition is found in another place in John's first epistle where he wrote that '...we receive from him anything we ask, because we obey his commands and do what pleases him...' (1 John 3:22). John states that two things will bring confident answers to prayer:

(a) obeying God's commands, which, in context, are not just his commands in general but the specific ones to believe in Jesus and love other Christians (v. 23).

(b) our motivation in obeying these commands is to please the Lord.

Phrased differently, if the inner drive of our life is to honour and glorify God by following Jesus and loving his people, we are positioning ourselves for answered prayer.

A fourth condition is found in Mark 11:24. Standing before the fig tree that had been cursed, Jesus addressed his astonished disciples by saying, 'Therefore I tell you, whatever you ask for in prayer, believe that you have received it, and it will be yours.' This fourth condition for answered prayer is 'faith'. To understand the pathology of the nature of faith described here, we must forensically trace back to the teaching found in the previous verses. In verses 22–23 Jesus told his disciples that:

- The *object* of their faith—the person they were to put their faith in—must be God alone (v. 22 'Have faith in *God*'). As we have previously seen, faith is a response to the revelation of God in Christ and the Scriptures.

- Faith must be verbalised (v. 23 '...if anyone *says* to this mountain...'). Faith is not *just* evidenced by what we believe in our hearts but *also* by what we *say*!

- Importantly, Jesus added that any inner doubt or unbelief must be subdued and silenced (v. 23 '...and *does not doubt in his heart* but believes...')

- Faith must be vocalised through prayer (v. 24 '...whatever you *ask* for in prayer...'). Prayer is a primary way we express our faith in God.

- Faith must be filled with an anticipation of imminent divine answers (v. 24 '...believe that you have *received* it...')

- The combination of faith–filled prayer expressing faith–filled words from a faith–filled heart will see the result: (v. 24 '...*it will be done for him.*')

We must see this verse in light of all the other Scriptures which teach on prayer. Obviously not all prayer has this absolute certainty of answers. Some prayer is asking, petition, seeking, knocking or desiring. Many times we just don't know what the answer or outcome will be because we surrender our prayers to the sovereign will of God. This is where praying the Scriptures comes into the equation. Prayer saturated in Scripture is more likely to produce authentic faith which fills us with a hope–filled expectation of answers.

To conclude this point and this chapter, we note that another compelling reason to pray the Scriptures is because God answers prayer!

CHAPTER TWO

How to Pray the Scriptures

In the previous chapter I proposed nine biblical reasons for *why* we should pray the Scriptures. Let's move on to the next question: *how* do we pray God's Word? This chapter will explore five ways of praying the Scriptures.

1. Praying the actual verse as our personal prayer

A first way of praying the Scriptures is to use a particular biblical passage as a personal prayer to God. The chosen verse or verses become the actual prayer we pray. When we can't find the right words to express our prayer, we can turn to the recorded and inspired words of Scripture *as* our prayer. In essence, the verses become the cry of *our* hearts, even though the words are in biblical language.

Some years ago I was facing a circumstance that I didn't feel I had the strength to endure, so I prayed Jehoshaphat's prayer in 2 Chronicles 20:12 '*...For we have no power to face this vast army that is attacking us. We do not know what to do, but our eyes are upon you.*' To me, at the time, Jehoshaphat's words captured the exact sentiment of my heart. I couldn't find better words to express my need for God.

Another way of using a verse as a personal prayer is to change the personal pronouns. I may pray, for example, Ephesians 3:16–17 as follows: 'I pray that out of *your* glorious riches *you* may strengthen *me* with power through *your* Spirit in *my* inner being, so that Christ may dwell in *my* heart through faith.'

Similarly, another option is to personalise the Scripture by substituting a name in Scripture with the name of the person we are praying for. For example, let's say we're praying for a new believer who is having trouble changing his old way of speaking. Brian swears and gossips but wants to change. So we pray Ephesians 4:29 for him: 'Do not let any unwholesome talk come out of *Brian's* mouth, but only what is helpful for building others up according to their needs, that it may benefit those who listen.' In this case we are using that very Scripture to pray more specifically for *Brian's* growth as a Christian and his personal renewal of thinking, character and behaviour (see Ephesians 4:20–24).

A further way of praying the Scriptures as a personal prayer is to use a paraphrase in contemporary English as a prayer. We might, for example, pray Paul's prayer in Colossians 1:9 as rendered by the Contemporary English Version, '...*that God will show you everything he wants you to do and that you may have all the wisdom and understanding that his Spirit gives.*' Or we may choose to use other people's prayers which are based on Scripture. There are many such prayers from the early church fathers, significant figures in church history or leaders in the contemporary church.

> As we are praying the words of Scripture, the verses become our personal prayer to God

Many Christian traditions encourage praying the Psalms. This is the most common and popular way to pray the Scriptures.

The Psalms are incredibly and insightfully expressive. The idea is to read the Psalm out as a prayer to God, then capture the essence of the passage by praying the general thrust of the passage—phrase by phrase—in our own words. Praying the Scriptures, however, doesn't have to be restricted to the Psalms alone—it could be any applicable passage.

The key thought here, though, is that as we are praying the words of Scripture, the verses become *our* personal prayer to God.

2. Use a passage or verse as a framework for our own prayers

A second way of praying the Scriptures is to structure our prayer times around a biblical passage which is meaningful or relevant for our circumstances at a particular time. We use the key thoughts, themes or applications of the passage as a basis for our prayers.

A classic example is Jesus' teaching on prayer (Matthew 6:9–13; Luke 11:1–4). In these passages Jesus was teaching his disciples *how* to pray. Jesus stated: 'This, then, is *how* you should pray' (Matthew 6:9). He was providing a *model* prayer around which they could *pattern* or *frame* their own prayers. This *pattern* prayer shouldn't be the only passage we pray, but it provides a model for using other biblical passages as a framework in our prayer times.

The 'Lord's Prayer' contains six petitions which follow the initial address to God as our Father. The first three concern God's name, God's kingdom and God's will. The last three concern our human needs. Sadly, we often reverse the order and begin with our needs rather than focus our prayers on God.

Using the version of Lord's Prayer found in Matthew 6 as our example, I will suggest some ideas for how it could be used as a framework to structure our time of prayer.

'Our Father in heaven…' (v. 9)

Begin each time of prayer by drawing near to God in intimacy. He is our Father and the Father of all who believe in him through Jesus Christ. Remember to maintain an attitude of reverence and awe because he is 'in heaven'.

Three heavenward petitions:

- '*...hallowed be your name...*' *(v. 9)*

    Worship, revere, honour and regard God and his name as holy.

- '*...your kingdom come...*' *(v. 10)*

    Pray that we may experience the reality of God's reign in the whole of our lives and in the fruitfulness and influence of the church as we anticipate his coming.

- '*...your will be done on earth as it is in heaven.*' *(v. 10)*

    Pray to fully surrender our will to his will with all of its implications.

Three human petitions

- '*Give us today our daily bread.*' *(v. 11)*

    Pray for the provision of what we need for each day but with a thankful attitude of dependence upon God.

- '*Forgive us our debts, as we also have forgiven our debtors.*' *v. 12; cf. vv. 14–15)*

    While asking God to forgive us for the sins we have committed against him, we must consciously forgive those who have sinned against us.

- '*And lead us not into temptation, but deliver us from the evil one.*' *(v. 13)*

    Pray that God would preserve us from being so susceptible to areas of weakness (temptation) and to resist Satan's influence, enticements and traps.

"...for yours is the kingdom and the power and the glory for ever. Amen."

Conclude the time of prayer with heartfelt worship of God for his eternal reign, power and glory.

This principle and process is not just helpful to our *personal* prayer times, but could also be applicable in our *public* prayer meetings. An example of using a passage as a framework around which to structure our prayer gatherings is Acts 4:23–31. After being threatened by the Sanhedrin, Peter and John returned to the church to report their whole experience. This caused a spontaneous eruption of loud corporate prayer. As we dissect their prayer in Acts 4 we note a structure that could be employed in a larger prayer service.

- *Declare the sovereignty of God* ('Sovereign Lord' v. 24)

    The first words the early church uttered were 'Sovereign Lord'. The application is to begin a prayer meeting by declaring the reign and sovereignty of God over all circumstances, including adverse ones.

- *Base the prayer on Scripture* ('You spoke by the Holy Spirit...' vv. 25–26; cf. Psalm 2:1–2)

    Before asking for anything, the early church declared Scriptures that related to their immediate needs. The lesson is to base our prayers on the Word of God by quoting passages relevant to the things being prayed for.

- *Centre our prayer on what Jesus has done on the cross* ('They did what your power and will had decided beforehand...' vv. 27–28)

    The early church regarded the conspiracy that led to Jesus' death as part of the predetermined, redemptive plan of God. We should equally centre all our prayer on the finished work of the cross.

- *Pray specifically* ('...consider their threats...enable your servants to speak with great boldness...stretch out your

hand to heal and perform miraculous signs and wonders...'
vv. 29–30)

> After declaring God's reign, proclaiming Scripture, exalting the cross, the early church were ready to make specific requests. Likewise we would be encouraged to pray comprehensively about the specific things we are asking God to do (Philippians 4:6–7).

- *Lifting up the name of Jesus* ('...through the name of your holy servant Jesus' v. 30)

> The church's bold requests were prayed in Jesus' name. In the same way, our prayers should be offered in the name of Jesus because it is through his name we have access to our loving Father in prayer (John 16:23–24; 26).

The result of their prayer was astonishing and dramatic. 'After they prayed, the place where they were meeting was shaken. And they were all filled with the Holy Spirit and spoke the word of God boldly' (v. 31). We, too, should expect mighty answers to prayer.

The process of using a passage as a framework for prayer is summed up in three easy steps:

- Devotionally read through a particular passage.

- Pause at the end of each verse to reflect on the principle or key thought embedded in the verse.

- Use that key thought as the basis for a response in prayer.

By way of example, we may be praying through Psalm 23. As we read the statement, '...*he restores my soul*' (from verse 3) we could draw out the thought that the Lord *our* shepherd is able to restore (revive,

> Praying the Scriptures provides us a greater insight into Scripture

renew) our inner being. Our prayerful response to this verse could then be to ask God to 'restore' our lives to inward wholeness and well–being. Then as we move on to the next part of the verse ('He guides me in paths of righteousness for his name's sake'), we may ask God to give us guidance so that our choices will ultimately bring glory to him.

In summary, praying the Scriptures potentially provides us a greater insight into the meaning and application of Scripture to our lives. It will also help us know more of God's Word.

3. Prayers of praise or thanksgiving

One very meaningful way to pray the Scriptures is to use a passage as an expression of thanksgiving or praise to God. As we read a portion of Scripture aloud or in our hearts, we lift up to God our worship, adoration or thanks. For example, we might pray Psalm 104:1 as a prayer of praise to God: *'Praise the Lord, O my soul. O Lord my God, you are very great; you are clothed with splendour and majesty.'*

> Praying the Scriptures is a practical way to foster an attitude of thankfulness and gratitude to God

Alternatively we may choose to rewrite the psalm or passage in our own words (or use the rendering of a modern paraphrase) so that it becomes a very personal, thoughtful and heartfelt prayer of thanksgiving or praise.

Or we may choose to pray a psalm (or any passage of Scripture), then respond to some of the phrases from our own personal experiences. If we were to declare, by way of example, Psalm 105:1: *'Give thanks to the Lord, call on his name; make known among the nations what he has done'*, we could respond to the last few words *'...what he has done'* by thanking God for the specific things he has done for us (such as the cross, forgiveness, life, family).

Praying the Scriptures in this way is a practical way to foster an attitude of thankfulness and gratitude to God (Philippians 4:6 and 1 Thessalonians 5:18).

4. Pray particular verses as a biblical basis for a specific prayer

A fourth way to pray the Scriptures is to use a particular verse or passage as the biblical basis for a specific request, petition or intercession. Our prayers are most effective when they are grounded on Scriptural principles.

A first step is to locate the verses that correlate with our needs or requests. There are numerous resources such as concordances, Bible encyclopaedias or study Bibles that list biblical topics and related verses. Then we thoughtfully reflect on each reference to discover what the verse teaches about the need or request we are praying about. The insights become the basis for our prayer.

For example, we may be going through a time of inner turmoil because of tension in the workplace or home. We may have a deep–seated need at these times for the peace of God. So we might turn to Philippians 4:6–7: *'Do not be anxious about anything, but in everything, by prayer and petition, with thanksgiving, present your requests to God. And the peace of God, which transcends all understanding, will guard your hearts and your minds in Christ Jesus.'* On the basis of this verse we could pray along the lines of: 'My Father, I thank you for your unfailing love and constant presence. From what I have just read in your Word (Philippians 4:6–7), I am specifically asking you to intervene in my circumstances and fill me with your peace. I need your peace within me so that I may go on. I ask you in Jesus' name and for his glory.'

This is a petition based on Scripture. There may be other things to pray about in the circumstances (such as reconciliation or resolution), but the predominant need may be for the peace of God as a starting point.

At times, it may be appropriate to do some personal study on the Scripture. Here are some practical ideas on how to do so:

- Look at the verses in context and read them in several versions to grasp the meaning.

- Pick out the key words and phrases and look up their meanings in a Word Study Book or a Bible Encyclopaedia.

- For those with the time and inclination, check the tense, prose and context of the passage. This will give great insight into interpreting the text.

- A further option is to consult a commentary which may provide specialist and scholarly perspective on the verse or passage.

- Maybe even check other places where the same word is used to flesh out its meaning in Scripture.

- Rewrite it in our own words as if we had to explain its meaning to someone who asked.

- Always apply it by writing out how this verse is applicable.

- Then use the insights as a basis for prayer.

Basing our prayers on Scripture is, as mentioned, more likely to align them with God's Word, will and ways. It also means that we are not asking for something based on our needs alone, but on God's Word.

5. Meditation

Meditation is a fifth way of praying the Scriptures. In Scripture, the word 'meditation' can mean 'ponder, muse, mutter or practise'. As a biblical concept, 'meditation' conveys the idea of reading a portion of Scripture in thoughtful, prayerful reflection (see Joshua 1:8; Psalm 1:2). In practical terms, this may mean reading and rereading the same passage many times over with the clear intention of 'thinking about, reflecting upon, considering, taking to heart, reading slowly and carefully, prayerfully taking in, and humbly receiving in mind, heart and will that which God has revealed'* in His Word.

The purpose of 'meditating' on Scripture is twofold. First, it is to gain insight (illumination / revelation) into the meaning concealed within the verses. It is to 'hear' the Spirit's voice speaking to our hearts and minds through the passage we're focusing on. Christian meditation brings comprehension and understanding that go beyond a cerebral level.

Secondly, a believer is encouraged to meditate on Scripture with the expressed purpose of drawing *application*—what we must do to *apply* this portion of God's Word to our lives. Moses' words to Joshua to (1:8) '...*meditate on it* [book of the law] *day and night, so that you may be careful to **do** everything written in it*' show that meditation should not only lead to insight (illumination / revelation) but also to its *application*.

Christian meditation is one of the ways in which we 'listen' to God's voice through his Word. It is a means by which we obtain comprehend the meaning of a verse. Also, meditation is a pathway to reflect on the implications and applications of the Scriptures to our lives. It is an 'inward digesting'** of the Word of God brought about by the Holy Spirit.

As part of a daily devotional engagement with God, read a passage with the purpose of thoughtful and prayerful reflection. Meditate to discover insight into the passage and application of its truth.

---

* Toon, Peter, *Meditating as a Christian*, London: Collins, 1991, p. 19.
** Ibid, p. 29.

CHAPTER THREE

Practical Ideas for Learning to Pray the Scriptures

Now that we've explored nine reasons *why* we should pray the Scriptures and five methods of *how* to do so, this chapter will examine some practical steps to get started.

Journaling

A very practical way to learn how to pray the Scriptures is to develop the practise of journaling each day. Journaling is a great way to have a 'conversation with God'. It becomes a record of our dialogue with God. God speaks to us through his Word. Our journal entry is our reply.

A simple way to approach journaling the Scriptures is through the use of the acrostic: SOAP. The individual letters in the word 'SOAP' represent four words that form a step by step method for journaling. They are:

S = Scripture

O = Observation

A = Application

P = Prayer

The process of journaling begins with us reading our Bibles every day. There are many methods people employ to read the Scripture such as:

- Bible reading guide—these guides provide a list of designated passages to read each day of the year

- Devotional book or daily email—this is a collection of thoughts or reflections from a Christian author for each day of the year. It normally contains suggested passages to read to complement the thought for that day.

- Systematic reading—this approach begins in Genesis 1:1 and keeps reading systematically until reaching Revelation 22:21—however long it takes.

- Chronological reading—this approach is to read through the Bible in the chronological order in which the events transpired.

There is no perfect method to read the Bible. One method is not right and another wrong. We may take some time in experimentation until we find a particular model of reading Scripture that works for us. The important principle is to read the Bible every day.

Before reading, we should always start with a brief prayer asking the Holy Spirit to speak to us through the Scriptures as we read. The Word of God has been divinely inspired, so we'll need divine help to understand it.

Then begin reading the Bible passages slowly, thoughtfully and expectantly.

When finished reading, ask some personal questions like:

- 'What verses or thoughts from this reading *spoke* to me?'

- 'What was particularly meaningful?'

- 'What do I sense God is saying to me through this passage?'
- 'What new insight did I see?'

After a few minutes of reflection we'll be ready to journal. This is where we use the word SOAP in the process of journaling.

For each new entry we need to write down the day's date on the top of the page. Please add the year because as we fill more and more journals we may quickly forget the year we wrote a particular entry.

S – *Scripture*

As a first step, we should record in our journal the actual words, phrases, verses or passage (however short or long) that particularly spoke to us. Write it out in full because this will reinforce its significance.

If time permits, maybe have a look at the verses or passage in other versions or paraphrases of Scripture. This may provide a different perspective on the verse. Some people like to rewrite the passage in their own words, so that it becomes a personal expression of what it meant to them.

O – *Observation*

Secondly, look at the whole reading for the day, then *briefly* observe what precedes and follows it. Like a single piece out of a jigsaw puzzle, the passage that *spoke* to us is part of a bigger picture. By making a few observations we will discover the bigger picture and where our 'piece' fits in. This is known as finding the 'context' of the passage. Ask some questions like: 'What is going on here? What is the author's train of thought? How does this section I'm focusing on fit into the overall flow of thought?'

Then briefly record your observations.

A – *Application*

This is the important bit. We then write down, thirdly, whatever lesson, encouragement, direction, correction or insight we have received from these verses. Ask some questions like: 'What was the lesson for my life? What do I need to do about what I have read? How did it come alive to me when I read it? Or what did I learn about God or his ways in this passage?'

Write the application down in an honest and personal way.

P – *Prayer*

Once we've recorded the verses (S), made some brief observations (O) and written our application (A), we respond to our selected passage from God's Word in prayer (P). At this point, we should thoughtfully record our prayer in the journal. This is a great way to capture the moment and, most importantly, to engage with God and his Word through prayer. Writing it down also gives us a record of what was happening in our heart at the time.

This is the elementary way in which we learn to pray the Scriptures. As we pray aloud the prayer recorded in our journal we are taking the first steps in learning how to pray the Scriptures.

Pray with a mature Christian who practices praying the Scriptures

Generally speaking, one of the best ways to learn how to pray is simply by praying, but another helpful way is by praying with other people who know how to pray. This same principle applies to praying the Scriptures. My encouragement, therefore, is to look for someone to mentor you in the exercise of praying the Scriptures.

Pray Scripture aloud

In some Christian traditions and orders, strong emphasis is given to contemplation and the disciplines of meditation, reflection, solitude, waiting and listening. In Charismatic and Pentecostal circles equal weight is given to the verbal confession and declaration of Scripture. Speaking God's Word aloud is a way of making a statement of personal faith in God and belief in his Word.

> Christians need their daily intake of God's Word for growth, sustenance and strength. Christians need to read their Bible every day

By way of example, we may be reading through the book of Hebrews by focusing on statements about Jesus, which we could then personalise and speak out loud as follows:

- *'I receive your grace and your mercy, and believe you will help me in my time of need'* (4:14–16).

- *'...because you live forever, Jesus, you have a permanent priesthood'* (7:24).

- *'Therefore, Jesus, you are able to save me completely...who come to God through you, because you always live to intercede for me'* (7:25).

- *'You are such a High Priest who meets my needs—One who is holy, blameless, pure, set apart from sinners, exalted above the heavens'* (7:26).

Speaking Scripture aloud edifies our inner person as the unchanging truth and power of God's Word fills our hearts and minds.

When should we pray the Scriptures?

The quick answer to this question is: every day!
One of the ways the Word of God is portrayed in Scripture is as nourishing and refreshing food (Hebrews 5:14; 1 Peter 2:2). Christians need their daily intake of God's Word for growth, sustenance and strength. Christians need to read their Bible *every day*. Similarly, praying the Scriptures should become a *daily* devotional exercise and a natural extension and expression of our daily engagement with God's Word. For those of us with a Bible reading guide, all we need to do is to add some extra time to take one of the most recent meaningful Scriptures and use it as a basis for prayer.

Another obvious opportunity to pray the Scriptures is in a time of uncertainty, challenge or crisis. Find the relevant verses and use them as a basis for prayer to endure and persevere through the difficulty.

Also, in every gathering of Christian people—whether a Church Eldership / Council / Board, Life Group or Worship Service—use a Scripture as a devotional reading, but also as a basis for a prayer for that meeting.

Where should we pray the Scriptures?

We can pray the Scriptures wherever or whenever we meet with God. Because of God's indwelling presence through the Holy Spirit we can engage with God anywhere at any time. It could be in the 'secret place' of private prayer or in a public prayer meeting. The most personal and pertinent place to pray the Scriptures is wherever we are communing with God in our personal devotions. Seize any and every opportunity to read and pray the Scriptures.

CLOSING COMMENT

The story is told of a young boy who was on his way to Kids' Church one Sunday morning. Before leaving, his mother gave him two dollar coins. 'This one,' said the mother as she placed a coin in his left hand, 'is to be put into the offering for God.' 'But this other one,' she continued as she placed the second coin in his right hand, 'is for you to buy some lollies on the way home.'

Very excitedly the little boy began walking toward the local church only a few hundred metres up the road. On the way, however, he tripped over an unseen rock protruding from the unsealed footpath. To brace his fall he instinctively spread out his hands, thus dropping the coins. Upon recovering his breath he found himself sprawled on the grass. To his horror he noticed the two coins were rolling toward a drain. He scrambled as fast as he could to intercept them.

As he dived, he just managed to place the ends of his fingers on one coin. Desperately he lunged for the other, but he was too late. It dropped into the drain and landed on the muddy bottom with a barely audible 'thud'. Carefully positioning himself over the drain, the boy looked down in despair at the coin which lay beyond his reach.

His gaze shifted up as he contemplated his next move. He looked at the sky, then at the coin lying in his open hand. Once again, he looked up, then again at the remaining coin. Finally he gave a deep sigh. 'Sorry, God, but that was *your* coin that fell down the drain!'

Tragically, many Christians utilise their time with God in a similar way. They use their discretionary time as this young boy used his remaining coin—for themselves. Their sentiment runs along the lines of: 'Sorry, God, but that was *your* time that I used for myself'— even though it may be with different words.

To really encounter God in prayer, and to grow in intimacy with him, demands the discipline of using our time wisely. Prayer is not easy. Admittedly, there are hundreds (if not thousands) of easier things to do with our time. On occasions, even when we are praying, we find it so much easier to simply pray about the immediate and pressing needs or requests in our life without any real thought, thankfulness or genuine engagement with God. We sometimes feel that we have done our 'duty'. Gnawing in our hearts, however, is a hunger and desire for a more authentic and meaningful prayer–life.

My challenge to every reader is to practice the principles in this book (especially chapter two) thoughtfully, slowly, diligently, patiently and expectantly. To do so, we must reprioritize our time, discipline our minds, still our hearts, treasure the moments we have with God and open the Scriptures as we pray. We are never alone on this journey of prayer. The Holy Spirit will lead us. As we ask him for help and seek him for guidance, we will experience his gentle and patient tutorship.

I want to conclude this short book by praying for you and your journey while you begin the adventure of praying the Scriptures.

Living and loving God, thank you for the 'new and living way' you made available through Jesus' shed blood by which we can now come close to you with boldness and confidence (Hebrews 10:19–20). *Lord, we choose to 'come near to you', knowing that as we do so you are drawing near to us* (James 4:8). *We worship you* (Psalm 95:6), *praise you* (Psalm 100), *give thanks to you* (Psalm 100:4; 1 Thessalonians 5:18), *and love you with all our heart, soul, mind and strength* (Matthew 22:37).

I pray for the readers of this book, Lord, that you would ignite a fresh passion for prayer in their hearts. May they persevere in prayer and not give up (Luke 18:1–8). *May they ask and keep on asking, seek and keep on seeking, knock and keep on knocking because I know that the person who asks receives, who seeks finds and to those who knock the door will be opened* (Luke 11:9–10).

May their prayers be grounded in your eternal Word! Empower each reader to live in obedience to your Word so they may receive answers to prayer (1 John 3:22). *Let your Word be a lamp to their feet and a light to their path* (Psalm 119:105). *May your Holy Spirit remind them of specific verses at appropriate times to use as a basis for prayer. By your Word may they 'stand their ground' through prayer in their spiritual battles* (Ephesians 6:17). *May they learn to meditate upon your Word every day to understand its' embedded truth and application* (Joshua 1:8). *As we read the Scripture let us 'hear' your voice speaking to us. Having heard your voice, may we respond to your Word with heartfelt prayer. Most of all, as each of us pray the Scriptures, may we gain greater understanding of, and intimacy with, the Living Word, our Saviour Jesus Christ* (John 1:14).

Lord God, may your presence fill our hearts as we reach out to you in prayer. May each reader love you more intensely, live for you more wholeheartedly, pursue you more vigorously, please you more intentionally and know you more deeply through praying the Scriptures.

I pray this in Jesus' name and for your eternal glory. Amen.

Recommended Reading:

Howard, Evan B., *Praying the Scriptures*,
Downers Grove, Ill: InterVarsity Press, 1999.

Kendall, RT. *Did You Think to Pray*,
London: Hodder and Stoughton, 2008.

Toon, Peter, *Meditating as a Christian*,
London: Collins, 1991.

About the Author

Pastor Bruce Hills (B Min, MA Theo)

Bruce has been in Christian ministry since 1984 and brings a wealth of experience and wisdom. He is known and respected around Australia for his prophetic and insightful preaching. One well known Christian leader in Asia described him as having the 'precision of a teacher, but the fire of a prophet'. With a passion for missions, Bruce frequently travels to many nations speaking at seminars and conferences. For nine years (2000–2009) Bruce pastored one of Australia's largest Pentecostal churches. He now serves as International Leadership Development Director for World Outreach International training and equipping pastors and leaders in the majority world. Bruce has been married to Fiona since 1983 and has three grown children. They live in Melbourne, Australia.

For more information on the author see www.brucehills.com.au and on World Outreach see www.world-outreach.com

What Others Are Saying About This Book ...

Rev. Bruce Hills' ministry and leadership have always been passionate, marked with clarity of teaching, keen prophetic insights with apostolic authority and inspiration. His book, *Praying with Power - How to Engage in a Deeper Level of Personal Prayer by Praying the Scriptures*, will inspire and lift your prayer life to a different level because; he has experienced the power of it through every season of his personal life and ministry.

Rev. Ong Sek Leang
General Superintendent, Assemblies of God of Malaysia and Senior Pastor, Metro Tabernacle, Malaysia

Pastor Bruce Hills has produced what I believe will be a very popular handbook on prayer. This is a must read for any who understand the importance and power of prayer, who want their prayer life to go to a whole new level. This easy to read book is a powerful tool that highlights simple principles that one can easily learn and apply.

John Elliott
International Director, World Outreach

Bruce Hills has authored a much-needed book on praying the scriptures. Many Christians struggle with daily prayer often because they see few answers. *Praying with Power,* shares great insights on how praying the scriptures will result in more answers to prayer. The clear practical guidelines along with compelling personal examples will inspire you to put "Praying the Scriptures" into practice.

Tak Bhana
Senior Minister, Church Unlimited, Auckland, NZ